Cooking Together

with
Chef Jean-Pierre

Cartoons by
John S. Milligan

JBM

D1800238

A Delightful Collection of Recipes Using Fish and Seafood

Cooking Together with Chef Jean-Pierre

Copyright © 1998 by JPJ Cookbooks
613-831-2413, 819-663-2479
fax: 819-663-5878

All rights reserved.

Except for reviews, no part of this book may be
reproduced without permission from the publisher.

Book Design: Wendelina O'Keefe

Printed By: Performance Printing Ltd.

Canadian Cataloguing in Publication Data

Ekobena, Jean-Pierre
    Cooking together with Chef Jean-Pierre

ISBN: 0-9683906-0-9

    1. Cookery (Fish). 2. Cookery (Seafood).
I. Milligan, John S. (John Stevenson), 1935- II. Title.

TX747.E46 1998   641.6'92   C98-900718-9

Cooking Together

This cookbook is the first in a series of "Cooking Together" cookbooks in which chef Jean-Pierre Ekobena has drawn from his years of experience as a chef in kitchens around the world, from Washington, D.C., Dakar, Senegal to Bonn, Germany and finally here in Ottawa. Born on May 11, 1951 in Yaounde, Cameroon, Jean-Pierre studied at Les Grandes Études Hotellières in France. His love for fish and seafood was nurtured and developed while preparing the catch of the day that came daily from the coasts of Brittany. For many years he was a chef at various embassies in Ottawa, and for five years the assistant chef at the Royal Ottawa Golf Club. Jean-Pierre Ekobena is a member of both the Canadian Federation of Chefs de Cuisine and the World Society of Cooks. He has published three previous cookbooks featuring African international cuisine. He has been the recipient of numerous culinary awards throughout his career, the most recent of which is the 1998 Recognition Award from the Canadian Federation of Chefs de Cuisine.

The concept for this cookbook series is based upon two assumptions. The first is that recipes do not have to be complicated to be good. The second is that enjoyment in cooking is greatly enhanced when cooking together with another person, young or old.

This particular "Cooking Together" edition is intended for fish lovers—or possibly future fish lovers! The condiments and spices used in recipes throughout are common fare in quality food stores. The clear and concise steps for each simple, yet tasteful fish or seafood recipe add to the pleasure of the cooking experience.

Aside from the flavourful pleasures experienced when eating fish, it is a healthy food because it contains omega-3 essential fatty acids. These fatty acids have been shown to be effective in preventing coronary disease and in boosting the immune and nervous systems. They also appear to be beneficial in maintaining optimal brain functions. So, when eating fish, you can enjoy the taste and help the body be healthy at the same time.

Cartoon illustrations are an integral part of the cookbook. They are drawn by John S. Milligan, Q.C., a retired lawyer, who has exchanged his steel nib for an illustrator's felt pen. The cartoons emphasize the idea that cooking should be an enjoyable experience and that cooking and chuckling at the same time can only heighten that experience.

Welcome to "Cooking Together."

Contents

Cooking Together...

Recipes

HEY! WE'RE NOT ON THE MENU TODAY!

Ginger Shrimp
Serves 4

32	medium shrimp, peeled and deveined	32
2 tbsp.	corn starch	30 mL
1/4 cup	soya sauce	50mL
1/3 cup	sesame oil	75 mL
1/3 cup	ginger, freshly grated	75 mL
	or	
1 1/2 tsp.	powdered ginger	7 mL
1/4 cup	lemon juice	50 mL
1 tbsp.	vegetable or olive oil	15 mL
1	clove garlic, crushed or sliced	1
1/8 tsp.	chili oil or hot sauce	0.5 mL

Combine corn starch with soya sauce,
stirring until well blended.

Add remaining ingredients, mixing well.

Marinate shrimp in mixture for 2 hours in refrigerator.

Remove from marinade and spear 4 shrimp on
each of 8 bamboo sticks.

Grill for 3 minutes per side.

Serve on a bed of rice.

Catfish with Lemon Cream

Serves 2

1	catfish fillet	1
1 tbsp.	butter	15 mL
	garlic salt	
	steak pepper	

In a pan, at medium-high heat, fry catfish fillet in butter for 5 to 6 minutes on each side.

Season with garlic salt and pepper. Cover for 5 seconds. Remove from pan and keep warm.

Lemon Cream

1 tbsp.	butter	15 mL
1	clove garlic, chopped	1
	juice of 1/2 lemon	
4 tbsp.	fresh cream (35%)	60 mL
2 tbsp.	white wine	30 mL
1 tsp.	corn starch	5 mL
1 tbsp.	chopped parsley	15 mL
	salt and pepper	

In a pan, at medium-high heat, sauté garlic in butter until soft.

Add lemon juice and reduce to desired consistency.

In a small bowl mix together fresh cream, white wine and corn starch.

Add mixture to pan, along with parsley.

Season with salt and pepper to taste.

Stir lemon cream mixture until thickened.

Pour into gravy boat or sauce dish and serve with fish.

NOW, THE BEST WAY IS TO PLACE THE HOOK IN THE WEEDS, THEN GIVE IT A TUG!

FLY STRIPPING CLASS

Salmon with Orange Butter

Serves 4

4	salmon fillets	4
3 tbsp.	butter	45 mL
1 tbsp.	olive oil	15 mL
4 tbsp.	chopped green onion	60 mL
4 tbsp.	fresh orange juice	60 mL
2 tbsp.	grated orange peel (zest)	30 mL
2 tbsp.	fish or seafood spice	30 mL
	salt and pepper	

Place fillets in an oven-proof casserole.

Melt butter and mix with remaining ingredients.

Pour on top of fillets.

Bake at 350°F (180°C) for 15 minutes.

Can also be wrapped in foil and cooked
on the barbecue.

Fish and Basil
Serves 2

2	fish fillets	2
1 tbsp.	basil-flavoured olive oil	15 mL
	or	
1 tbsp.	<u>each</u> olive oil and dried basil	15 mL
	juice of 1/2 lemon	
	steak pepper	
	garlic salt	
1 tsp.	chopped parsley	5 mL

Place fillets in glass dish or casserole.

Mix all remaining ingredients and pour over fish.

Marinate for 1 hour in refrigerator.

Remove fish from marinade, reserving marinade mixture.

In a pan, at medium-high heat, fry fish for 5 to 6 minutes each side. Remove from pan and keep warm.

Add the marinade mixture to pan and cook for 10 seconds.

Pour mixture over fish and serve immediately.

Grilled Halibut

Serves 2

1	halibut steak, 3/4" (2cm) thick	1
1 tbsp.	olive oil	15 mL
1 tbsp.	vinegar	15 mL
1 tsp.	lemon juice	5 mL
	garlic salt	
	black pepper	
1/4 tsp.	rosemary	1 mL

In a flat dish, combine all ingredients except halibut steak.

Place halibut in dish and marinate for 30 minutes at room temperature, turning occasionally.

Remove the halibut from marinade, reserving marinade mixture.

Place the steak on an oiled, pre-heated grill.

Cook for 5 to 6 minutes on each side, basting regularly with marinade mixture.

Fresh Water Cod Fillets

(microwave)
Serves 4

2 lbs.	cod fillets	1 kg
3/4 cup	orange juice	200 mL
1 tbsp.	lemon juice	15 mL
1 tbsp.	butter	15 mL
1 tbsp.	flour	15 mL
1/2 cup	fresh cream (35%)	125 mL
1 tbsp.	chopped fresh basil	15 mL
1 1/2 tsp.	chicken broth	7 mL
2 tbsp.	white wine	30 mL
	garlic salt	
	pepper	

Roll each cod fillet and place in a microwaveable dish.

Cover with waxed paper and microwave on High for 2 minutes.

Remove fillets from dish and keep warm.

Add remaining ingredients to dish, stirring constantly.

Microwave on High, uncovered, for 2 minutes.

Pour sauce over fillets and serve with quartered oranges and fresh basil.

Lemon Fish
Serves 4

2 lbs.	fresh fish	1 kg
6 tbsp.	vegetable oil	90 mL
4 tbsp.	lemon juice	60 mL
1 tsp.	grated lemon peel (zest)	5 mL
3 tbsp.	soya sauce	45 mL
1	clove garlic, crushed	1
1 tsp.	salt	5 mL
1/2 tsp.	rosemary	2 mL
1/2 tsp.	pepper	2 mL

Place fish pieces in flat glass dish or casserole.

In a bowl, mix together all remaining ingredients.

Pour mixture over fish and marinate for 1 hour in the refrigerator.

Remove fish from marinade.

On the barbecue or in a pan, grill or fry fish, at medium-high heat, for 4 to 6 minutes on each side.

Orange Whole Trout

(microwave)   Serves 4

1	whole trout (approximately 2 lbs./1 kg)	1
3/4 cup	orange juice	200 mL
1 tbsp.	lemon juice	15 mL
1 tbsp.	butter	15 mL
1 tsp.	flour	5 mL
3/4 cup	fresh cream (35%)	200 mL
1 tbsp.	chopped fresh basil	15 mL
	salt and pepper	

Garnish

2	oranges, peeled and quartered	2
	fresh basil leaves (optional)	

Place the whole trout in a microwaveable dish. Add orange juice and lemon juice.

Cover with waxed paper and cook on High for 3 minutes. Set aside, removing the fish from the dish to a serving dish, and reserving juice mixture.

In a small bowl, melt butter for 30 seconds. Add flour and reserved juice mixture.

Stirring constantly, add fresh cream, basil, and salt and pepper to taste.

Cook, uncovered, on High for 3 minutes, stirring frequently until thickened.

Pour mixture over fish and garnish with oranges and basil. Serve immediately.

PATIENCE!

Mussels

Serves 4

5 lbs.	mussels	2.5 kg
2	dried shallots or 1 onion, chopped	2
1 tbsp.	chopped parsley	15 mL
1/4 cup	lemon juice	50 mL
1	garlic clove	1
1/2 cup	dry white wine	125 mL
	pepper	
1/2 cup	fresh cream (35%)	125 mL

Scrub mussels well with a stiff brush. Discard any open mussels. (Squeeze the shell; if it opens even slightly, throw it away.) Trim off the beard (threadlike material) with scissors.

In a large pan, combine all ingredients except fresh cream.

Cover and cook until the shells open. (Discard any mussels that do not open.)

Strain and save the liquid, placing mussels in a serving dish.

Place liquid back in pan and cook on stove at medium-high heat until volume is reduced by approximately 2/3.

Add fresh cream and cook the sauce to a smooth consistency.

Pour the sauce over mussels and serve.

Catfish with Summer Herbs

Serves 4

2 lbs.	catfish fillets	1 kg
1 tbsp.	corn oil	15 mL
	salt and pepper	
1 tbsp.	butter	15 mL
1 tbsp.	chervil	15 mL
1 tbsp.	parsley	15 mL
1 tsp.	chives	5 mL
	juice of 1/2 lemon	

Heat oil in frying pan until very hot. Add catfish and cook on high for 3 minutes on each side, seasoning with salt and pepper to taste.

Remove fish from pan and keep warm on serving dish.

Return pan to heat. Melt butter.

Add chervil, parsley and chives.

Cook 1 minute. Add lemon juice.

Pour mixture over catfish. Serve immediately.

Lime Salmon or Trout
Serves 4

2 lbs.	salmon or trout fillets	1 kg
1 tbsp.	butter	15 mL
1 tbsp.	olive oil	15 mL
1/2	green pepper, chopped	1/2
1/2	red pepper, chopped	1/2
2	limes	2
1 tbsp.	finely chopped chives	15 mL
	salt and pepper	

Melt butter in large pan on medium-high heat for 1 minute. Add olive oil. Fry fish fillets for 30 seconds per side. Remove fish from pan, arrange on serving dish and keep warm in oven set at 200°F (90°C).

Grate the peel (zest) of both limes. Remove white membrane of one lime before slicing thinly. Squeeze the juice of the second lime into the melted butter in pan.

Add green and red peppers and cook for 30 seconds.

Add sliced lime, lime peel, and finely chopped chives and salt and pepper to taste.

Pour lime mixture over warm fish fillets. Serve immediately.

Chives Salmon
Serves 2

1/4 to 1/2 lb.	salmon fillet	125 to 250 g
2 tbsp.	butter	30 mL
1 tbsp.	olive oil	15 mL
1 cup	fresh cream (35%)	250 mL
1/2 cup	light cream	125 mL
1 tsp.	chopped chives	5 mL
1	garlic clove	1
2/3 cup	white wine (optional)	150 mL
1 tsp.	corn starch	5 mL
	black pepper	
	salt	
	chopped parsley	

In a frying pan, at medium-high heat, melt butter. Add olive oil. Cook salmon for 2 to 3 minutes each side. Remove salmon from pan and keep warm in oven set at 200°F (90°C).

In pan, lightly sauté garlic. Add wine if desired.

Mix the two creams together with chives and corn starch. Pour into pan and bring mixture to a boil, reducing heat quickly to simmer for 30 to 60 seconds.

Add parsley, salt and pepper. Pour over salmon.

This is ideal served with fettuccini.

Scallops Sweetheart
Serves 2

1/2 lb.	sea scallops	250 g
1 cup	skim milk	250 mL
2 tbsp.	flour	30 mL
1 tbsp.	olive oil	15 mL
1/2 cup	white wine	125 mL
1/2 cup	chopped shallots	125 mL
2 tbsp.	chopped green onion	30 mL
2 tsp.	fresh chopped parsley	10 mL
	lemon juice	
	pepper to taste	

With a cleaver, flatten scallops. Dip in skim milk and roll in flour.

Sauté scallops at medium-high heat in olive oil in a skillet for approximately 2 minutes.

Transfer scallops to a serving dish.

Pour white wine into skillet. Add shallots, green onion and parsley.

Simmer wine mixture for a minute or so and pour over scallops in serving dish.

Season with lemon juice and pepper. Serve.

Sautéed Scallops

Serves 2

1/2 lb.	scallops	250 g
2 tbsp.	olive oil	30 mL
1	garlic clove, crushed	1
4	dwarf corn on the cob	4
2 oz.	sugar peas	60 g
1	red pepper, sliced	1
1/2 lb.	bean sprouts	250 g
1 tbsp.	chicken broth	15 mL
1 tbsp.	white wine (optional)	15 mL
2 tbsp.	soya sauce	30 mL
1 tbsp.	corn starch	15 mL
	salt and pepper	

In a pan at medium-high heat, heat oil and sauté garlic lightly.

Add scallops and cook for 3 minutes, stirring frequently.

Add corn, sugar peas and red pepper. Cook for 1 minute.

Add the bean sprouts, chicken broth and wine.

Mix the soya sauce with corn starch and add to pan. Cook for 2 minutes until sauce thickens.

Add salt and pepper to taste. Serve.

Orange Roughy Fillets in Garlic Butter

Serves 4

4	orange roughy fillets	4
	salt or garlic salt	
	pepper	

Season with salt or garlic salt and pepper. Cook on grill or in pan over medium heat for 3 to 4 minutes each side.

Garlic Butter

1/2 lb.	butter, softened	250 g
2 tbsp.	chopped parsley	30 mL
1 tsp.	chervil	5 mL
5	garlic cloves, chopped	5
1 tbsp.	dry white wine	15 mL
1/4 cup	lemon juice	50 mL
	salt and pepper	

Mix all ingredients together. Roll in foil paper and keep in the refrigerator.

For presentation, put a slice of garlic butter on each fillet.

Garnish with lemon slices.

Salmon or Tilapia Fillets with Dill Sauce

Serves 4

4	salmon or tilapia fillets	4
1/2 cup	vegetable oil	125 mL
1/2 cup	lemon juice	125 mL
	salt or garlic salt	
	pepper	

Mix together oil, lemon juice and seasonings.

Pour over fillets to marinate for 30 minutes.

Remove fillets from marinade and dry out with paper towel.

On a grill or in a pan, at medium-high heat, fry fillets for approximately 3 minutes on each side.

Serve with dill sauce.

Dill Sauce

1 cup	sour cream or plain yogurt	250 mL
1/4 cup	fresh dill	50 mL
2 tbsp.	horseradish	30 mL
2 tbsp.	olive oil	30 mL

Mix together all ingredients and refrigerate for 2 hours before serving.

Salmon with Lemon Cream

Serves 4

1 1/2 to 2 lbs.	salmon fillets	700 g to 1 kg
	steak pepper	
	salt	

Lemon Cream

	juice of 1 lemon	
6 tbsp.	fresh cream (35%)	90 mL
4 tbsp.	white wine	60 mL
1 tsp.	corn starch	5 mL
1 tbsp.	chopped parsley	15 mL
1	garlic clove, chopped	1
4 tbsp.	butter	60 mL
1 tbsp.	olive oil	15 mL
	salt and pepper	

In a pan, at medium-high heat, fry fillets in half the butter and the 1 tbsp. (15 mL) olive oil for 5 to 6 minutes on each side. Season with steak pepper and salt.

Cover for 5 seconds before serving.

Meanwhile, place the remaining butter in another pan. Add garlic to sauté.

Add lemon juice and reduce.

Mix together fresh cream, white wine and corn starch. Add to lemon mixture.

Add parsley, salt and pepper and let thicken.

Pour into a gravy boat or sauce dish and serve with salmon.

Broiled Swordfish
or Tuna with Tomato Sauce

Serves 4 (photo, page 30)

4	swordfish or tuna steaks	4
1 tbsp.	shallots, minced	15 mL
1 1/2 tsp.	chopped garlic in olive oil	7 mL
1/2 cup	lime juice	125 mL

Place steaks in a glass casserole dish large enough to hold fish in a single layer.

Combine minced shallots with garlic and lime juice in a small bowl.

Pour over fish and marinate, covered, for half an hour.

Preheat broiler or grill and lightly oil the broiling pan or grill.

Cook steaks for 5 minutes on each side.

Serve with your favourite commercial tomato sauce.

Pork Fillet and Lobster Tails with Maple Sauce

See recipe, page 40

(PHOTO: BRUNO LAMARCHE)

Broiled Swordfish
with Tomato Sauce
See recipe, page 28

(PHOTO: BRUNO LAMARCHE)

Grilled Split Lobster

See recipe, page 48

(PHOTO: BRUNO LAMARCHE)

Stuffed Salmon or White Fish with Tomatoes
See recipe, page 62

(PHOTO: BRUNO LAMARCHE)

Poached Salmon Steaks

(microwave)
Serves 4 to 6

4 to 6	salmon steaks	4 to 6
1 tbsp.	olive oil	15 mL
	juice of 1 lemon	
	grated peel (zest) of 1/2 lemon	
6	peppercorns, crushed	6
1 tbsp.	salt	15 mL
1	onion, quartered	1

Place salmon steaks in a greased microwaveable dish.

Add lemon juice and peel.

Sprinkle with crushed peppercorns. Add onions.

Sprinkle salt in the juice around the fish.

Cover and poach on High for 2 minutes per fish piece (eg., 8 minutes for 4; 12 minutes for 6).

Let stand for 10 minutes.

Remove cover and let cool off slightly in the juices.

Remove from dish and place on a serving plate.

Salmon Fillets with Pineapple

Serves 4

4	salmon fillets 10 oz. (300 g) each	4

Pineapple Sauce

1 cup	fresh or canned pineapple, crushed	250 mL
2	green onions, chopped	2
1 tbsp.	lemon juice	15 mL
2 tbsp.	chopped fresh mint	30 mL
1 tsp.	chopped parsley	5 mL
1/2	garlic clove, crushed	1/2
1 tbsp.	olive oil	15 mL
	salt and pepper	

On a grill or in a pan at medium-high heat, cook salmon fillets for 3 to 4 minutes on each side.

In a blender, purée all remaining ingredients together. Serve at room temperature with salmon fillets.

Fish Fillets with Ginger
(microwave)
Serves 2

1 lb.	fish fillets of your choice	500 g
2 tbsp.	soya sauce	30 mL
	grated peel (zest) of 1 lemon	
1 tbsp.	lemon juice	15 mL
1 tbsp.	ketchup	15 mL
1	garlic clove, chopped	1
1 tbsp.	chopped fresh ginger	15 mL

In a microwaveable dish, mix soya sauce, lemon peel and juice, ketchup, garlic and ginger.

Cut the fish fillets into serving-size pieces. Place in sauce and turn to cover thoroughly.

Cover dish with waxed paper. Cook on High for 5 to 6 minutes or until fish flakes easily with fork.

Let stand, uncovered, for 5 minutes.

Serve fish with sauce.

Sole with Sour Cream

(microwave)
Serves 2

1 lb.	fillets of sole	500 g
1 cup	sour cream	250 mL
1/2 cup	chopped green onions	125 mL
1/2 tsp.	salt	2 mL
1/4 tsp.	pepper	1 mL
1 tsp.	basil	5 mL
1/2 cup	grated parmesan cheese	125 mL
	paprika	

Place the fish in a large, oiled microwaveable dish.

Mix together remaining ingredients, except paprika, and spread on fish.

Sprinkle with paprika.

Cover with waxed paper.

Cook at Medium for 6 minutes.

Let stand 5 minutes before serving.

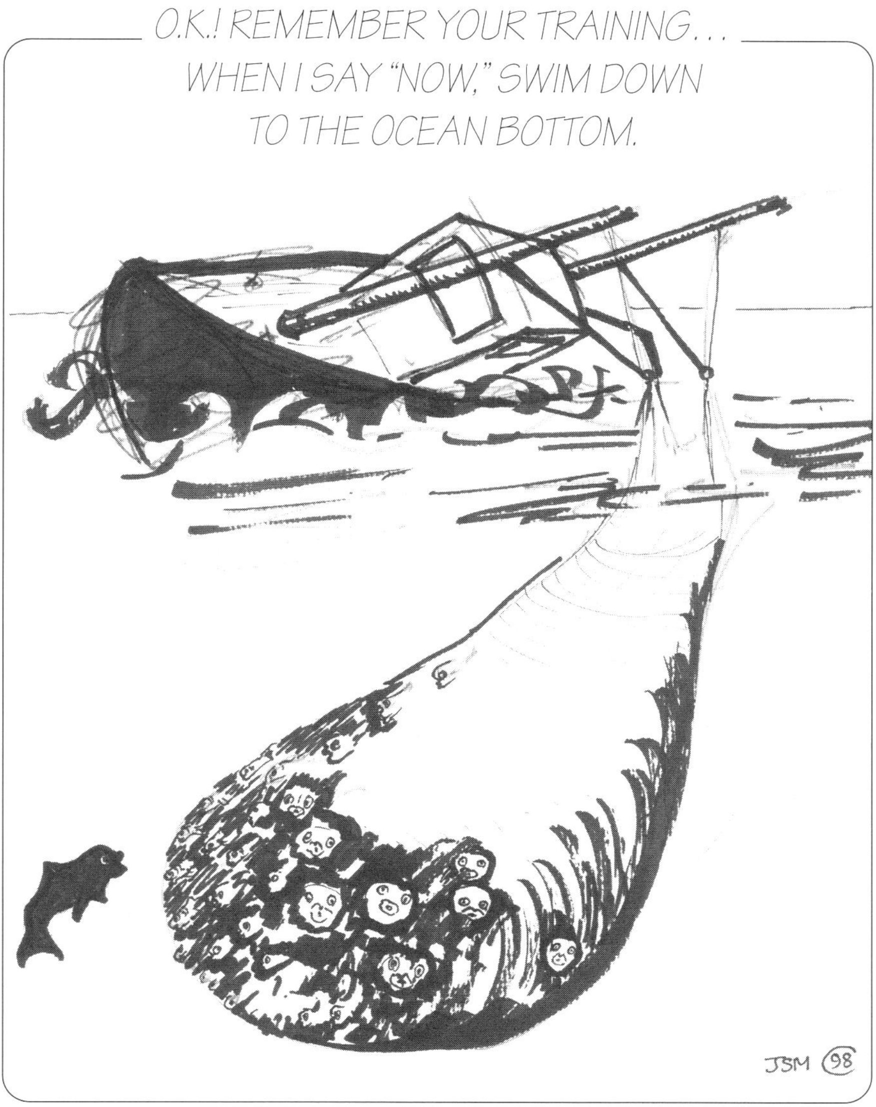

"School of Herring Drags Boat to Bottom"
Ottawa Citizen, Wednesday, January 7, 1998, pg. A6

Pork Fillet and Lobster Tails with Maple Sauce

Serves 4 (photo, page 29)

4	medallions of pork fillet (4 oz./125 g each)	4
	garlic salt	
	pepper	
4 tbsp.	butter	60 mL
1 tsp.	flour	5 mL
2 tbsp.	rosé wine	30 mL
10 tbsp.	pure maple syrup	150 mL
2 tbsp.	wine vinegar	30 mL
1 1/2 cups	chicken stock	375 mL
4	lobster tails	4
2 tbsp.	fresh parsley	30 mL
2 tbsp.	tomato paste	30 mL
1	clove of garlic, chopped	1

Season pork steaks with garlic salt and pepper.

In a large skillet, over medium heat, melt 2 tbsp. butter and sauté pork on both sides for 15 - 20 minutes until juices run clear when pork is pierced with a skewer.

Remove from skillet, set aside and keep warm.

Drain fat from skillet.

Add garlic and flour and cook until brown.

Add tomato paste, rosé wine and chicken stock to skillet and bring to boil, scraping up residues from base of skillet.

Add maple syrup, wine vinegar, and return to boil.

Reduce by one half.

Set aside and keep warm.

In a large sauce pan, poach lobster tails in barely simmering water for 4 - 5 minutes.

Drain well, set aside and keep warm.

Whisk remaining butter into sauce until melted.

Adjust seasoning to taste.

Spoon sauce onto plates, arranging a pork fillet and lobster tail on top of the sauce.

Pike with Sour Cream

(microwave)
Serves 4

2 lb.	whole pike, cleaned, but not cut	1 kg
1 tsp.	salt	5 mL
1/2 tsp.	pepper	2 mL
1 cup	sour cream	250 mL
1/2 cup	grated cheddar cheese	125 mL
1/4 cup	fresh dill	50 mL
	paprika	

Make 4 to 5 incisions on each side of fish and place in a large, well-greased microwaveable dish.

Season the inside of the fish with salt and pepper.

Mix together the sour cream, cheddar cheese and dill to form a paste.

Cover the top and sides of the fish with the paste. Sprinkle generously with paprika.

Cook, uncovered, on Medium-High for 6 to 8 minutes.

Remove from the microwave and cover with foil wrap. Let stand for 5 minutes.

Sprinkle with dill and serve.

Sole Fillet with Ginger and Lime

Serves 4

4	sole fillets	4
1 tbsp.	fresh ginger, grated	15 mL
1/4 cup	melted butter	50 mL
1/2 cup	chicken broth	125 mL
2 tsp.	fresh lime juice	10 mL
1/4 tsp.	lime peel (zest)	1 mL
	garlic salt	
	pepper	

Mix together all ingredients, except for fish.

In a pan, spread this mixture on top of sole fillets .

Cover and bake at medium-high heat for 7 minutes.

Serve with rice and green salad.

Selected Shellfish
Stew with Sauterne
Serves 2

3/4 lb.	fresh cooked shellfish	375 g
	(lobster, shrimp or crab)	
1 quart	whole milk	1 L
2 oz.	butter	60 g
	salt and pepper	
1/4 cup	dry sauterne wine	50 ml
1 tbsp.	chopped parsley	15 mL
	paprika	

Cut shellfish into fairly large cubes 1" (2.5 cm) square. Set aside.

Half fill the lower section of a double boiler with boiling water. Pour milk into the top section, adding butter, and salt and pepper to taste.

Heat milk, but do not bring it to the boiling point.

Add shellfish cubes to hot milk mixture. Now bring mixture to the boiling point, but do not boil.

Add sauterne wine. Heat for 1 minute.

Serve piping hot in pre-heated bowls. Sprinkle each with chopped parsley and a dash of paprika.

Haddock Scalloped au Gratin

Serves 2

1 lb.	haddock fillets	500 g
2 oz.	butter or margarine	60 g
1/2	green pepper, minced	1/2
1/2	onion, minced	1/2
1/2 tsp.	salt	2 mL
1/8 tsp.	pepper	0.5 mL
1/2 cup	grated or crumbled cheddar cheese	125 mL
2 cups	cracker crumbs	500 mL
1 cup	whole milk	250 mL
2 tbsp.	flour	30 mL
1/2 tsp.	Worcestershire sauce	2 mL

Wipe fillets with a damp cloth and cut into cubes.

Melt butter in a saucepan.

Add green pepper, onion, haddock cubes, and salt and pepper. Sauté gently over low heat for 10 minutes or until green pepper is half cooked.

Meanwhile, blend cold milk and flour in a mixing bowl. When very smooth, pour mixture into the top of a double boiler and cook for approximately 10 minutes until sauce begins to thicken.

Stir in Worcestershire sauce; then add sautéed haddock cubes and vegetables.
Pour mixture into a greased casserole dish.

Combine cheddar cheese with cracker crumbs and spread on top of casserole.

Bake, uncovered, in pre-heated 300° F (150°C) oven for 10 minutes or until golden brown.

Garnish with sprigs of mint, if desired.

Grilled Split Lobster

Serves 4 (photo, page 31)

1	cooked lobster	1
3 tbsp.	garlic butter (recipe, page 24)	45 mL
2 tbsp.	bread crumbs	30 mL

Cut the lobster in half lengthwise.

Remove the coral part.

Spread garlic butter on each half.

Sprinkle with bread crumbs.

Bake in a preheated, 400° F (200°C) oven for 3 - 4 minutes.

Garnish with lemon wedges and serve immediately.

The same recipe can be prepared with fresh lobster. Just cook it for 5 minutes in boiling water.

Zesty Stuffed Mussels
Serves 2

1 lb.	same-day fresh mussels (about 3 dozen)	500 g
2 tbsp.	sour cream	30 mL
2 tbsp.	mayonnaise	30 mL
1 tbsp.	dry white wine	15 mL
1 tsp.	Dijon mustard	5 mL
1 tsp.	finely chopped chives	5 mL

Scrub mussels well with a stiff brush. Discard any open mussels. (Squeeze the shell; if it opens even slightly, throw it away.) Trim off the beard (threadlike material) with scissors.

Steam mussels for 3 to 5 minutes or until they open. (Discard any mussels that do not open.)

Remove half of shell. Cool mussels.

Mix remaining ingredients and spoon 1/2 tsp. (2 mL) over each mussel. Serve.

Fresh drained oysters may also be used.

Lobster Herb Stuffing

Serves 6.

This is a wonderful stuffing for any kind of fish.

5 lbs.(approximately)	whole fish	2.5 kg
1 cup	cooked lobster meat	250 mL
1/4 cup	butter	50 mL
2	shallots, minced	2
1/4 tsp.	sage	1 mL
1/4 tsp.	thyme	1 mL
1	stalk celery	1
1/4 cup	sherry wine	50 mL
1/2	clove garlic, minced	1/2
1/2 tsp.	salt	2 mL
1/8 tsp.	pepper	0.5 mL
1	egg, beaten	1
3 cups	dry bread crumbs	750 mL
	paprika	

Melt butter in saucepan over medium heat.

Add shallots, sage, thyme, celery, garlic, salt, pepper, and pinch of paprika; sauté 5 minutes, or until shallots are soft.

Meanwhile, mince lobster meat; place in large mixing bowl.

In separate mixing bowl mix bread crumbs and well-beaten egg.

Mix together sautéed shallot mixture, bread crumbs and lobster meat; mix thoroughly.

Add enough sherry to moisten slightly; mix well. Stuff fish with mixture and sew shut.

Bake in a 400°F (200°C) oven for 35 - 45 minutes. After 40 minutes, check using a toothpick. If, after piercing the fish, the toothpick comes out dry, the fish is cooked.

For smaller fish, reduce amounts given here.

ETHEL. DO YOU THINK THAT HE IS GETTING ANXIOUS?

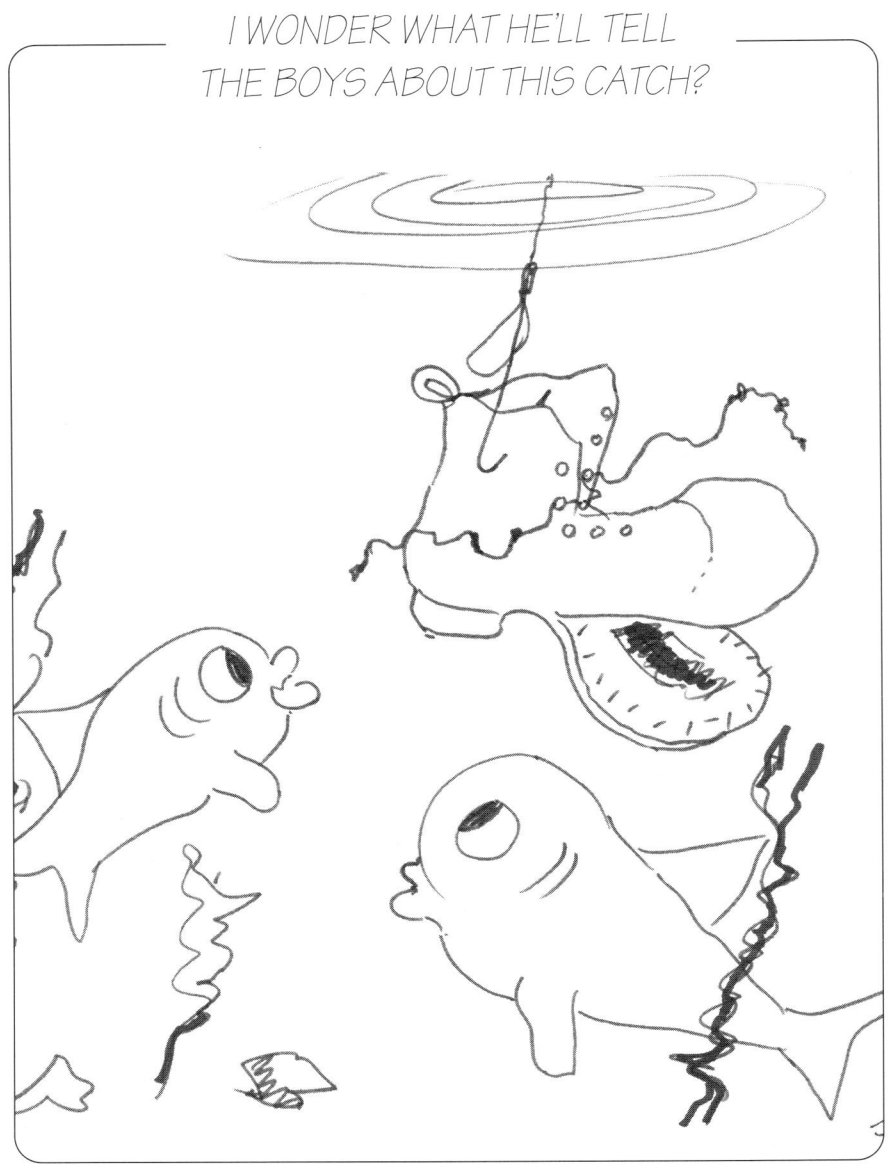

Herb-Baked Catfish

Serves 4

2 lbs.	catfish fillets	1 kg
2 tbsp.	butter or margarine, melted	30 mL
1	medium garlic clove, minced	1
1/2 tsp.	pepper	2 mL
1 tsp.	salt	5 mL
3/4 tsp.	paprika	4 mL
1/2 tsp.	dried thyme	2 mL
1/2 tsp.	dried basil	2 mL
1/2 tsp.	dried oregano	2 mL
2 tbsp.	lemon juice	30 mL
2 tbsp.	chopped parsley (optional)	30 mL

Combine garlic and melted butter. Spread evenly over the bottom of an 13" x 9" x 2" (33 x 23 x 5 cm) baking dish.

Combine pepper, salt, paprika, thyme, basil and oregano. Sprinkle herb mixture on both sides of catfish fillets.

Arrange fillets on top of melted butter and garlic. Drizzle with lemon juice.

Bake at 350°F (180°C) for 15 to 18 minutes or until fish is almost done.

Move the baking dish to between 4 and 6 inches (10 and 15 cm) from broiler element and broil for 4 to 6 minutes longer or until fish flakes easily with a fork.

Remove fish to a serving platter and top with pan juices. Garnish with parsley if desired.

Fish Chowder

Serves 6

1/2 lb.	salt pork	250 g
3	large onions, coarsely chopped	3
6	small potatoes, peeled and diced	6
2 1/4 lb.	haddock or cod fillets	1.125 kg
2 tbsp.	flour	30 mL
4 1/2 cups	milk	1.1 L
	salt	
	dash thyme	
	freshly ground pepper	

Remove any rind from the salt pork and discard.

Dice the pork and fry in a large saucepan until golden.

Remove the pork with a slotted spoon and drain on absorbent paper.

Brown the onions in the pork fat.

Meanwhile, in a Dutch oven, boil the potatoes for 5 minutes in just enough water to cover.

Cut the fish into 1 1/2 inch (4 cm) pieces and add to the Dutch oven.

Pour off any fat remaining in the saucepan.

Sprinkle the flour into the saucepan and stir in the milk, thyme, salt and pepper to taste.

Pour mixture into the Dutch oven, cover and simmer over low heat for 1 1/2 hours without stirring.

Season to taste and sprinkle with the reserved, browned salt pork just before serving.

Garlic Catfish Bouillabaisse

Serves 4

1 1/2 lbs.	catfish fillets, cut into cubes	750 g
1/4 cup	olive or vegetable oil	50 mL
4	medium onions, cut into 1/4" (0.65 cm) slices	4
4	large garlic cloves, thinly sliced	4
5	fish bouillon cubes	5
5 cups	water	1.2 L
2 cups	dry white wine	500 mL
16 oz.	can of diced tomatoes	500 mL
	cayenne pepper to taste	
1/2 tsp.	saffron threads or turmeric	2 mL
1 tsp.	dried thyme	5 mL
	1 bay leaf	
	salt and pepper	
2	large potatoes, peeled and cubed	2
3	medium carrots, sliced	3

Heat oil over medium heat in a large, heavy pan or Dutch oven.

Add onion and garlic. Cook until tender, stirring frequently.

Dissolve bouillon cubes in 5 cups (1.2L) of water. Add to onion mixture.

Stir in wine, undrained tomatoes, cayenne, saffron (or turmeric), thyme, bay leaf, and salt and pepper to taste. Bring to a boil.

Reduce heat. Cover and simmer for 5 minutes.

Add potatoes and carrots. Cover and simmer until vegetables are tender (about 12 minutes).

Add cubed catfish fillets. Cover and simmer for an additional 10 minutes.

Remove bay leaf and discard.

Serve in individual bowls.

Almond Trout
Serves 4

6	trout fillets	6
4 tbsp.	flour	60 mL
2 tbsp.	olive or vegetable oil	30 mL
2 tbsp.	butter	30 mL
3 tbsp.	slivered almonds	45 mL
1 tsp.	chopped parsley	5 mL
2 tbsp.	white wine	30 mL
1 tbsp.	lemon juice	15 mL
	salt and pepper	

Cover the trout fillets with flour. Shake gently to remove any excess flour.

In a pan, heat oil at medium-high heat. Cook the fillets for 3 to 4 minutes on each side. Remove fillets and place them in a serving dish.

In the same pan, heat butter. Add the almonds and cook for 1 to 2 minutes.

Add the wine, lemon juice, parsley, and salt and pepper to taste.

Pour the sauce over the fillets in the serving dish. Garnish with lemon slices and parsley.

Stuffed Fish Fillets
Serves 4

1 tbsp.	butter	15 mL
1 tbsp.	olive oil	15 mL
1	green pepper, cut into small pieces	1
4 tbsp.	onions, chopped	60 mL
4 tbsp.	almonds, sliced	60 mL
1/2 cup	bread crumbs	125 mL
1/2 tsp.	oregano	2 mL
4 tbsp.	lemon juice	60 mL
1 tbsp.	fresh coriander or parsley, chopped	15 mL
1 tsp.	salt	5 mL
4	fish fillets	4
2 cups	water	500 mL
2	garlic cloves	2
1 tsp.	pepper	5 mL

In a frying pan, at medium-high heat, melt butter. Add olive oil and sauté the green peppers and half of the onions until the peppers are soft and the onions golden.

Add almonds, bread crumbs, oregano, 1 tbsp. (15 mL) lemon juice, coriander and salt. Mix well.

Spread mixture on centre of each fish fillet, roll and secure with a toothpick.

In an oven-proof casserole, add the rest of the onions, water, garlic, pepper and the remainder of the lemon juice.

Place the rolled fillets into the casserole and bake in a preheated 400°F (200°C) oven for 30 to 35 minutes.

Grilled Lobster Tails

Serves 4

4	frozen lobster tails	4
1/4 cup	butter or margarine, melted	50 mL
1 tbsp.	lemon juice	15 mL
1/2 tsp.	grated lemon peel (zest)	2 mL
	dash ginger	
	dash paprika	
	garlic salt	
	pepper	

Partially thaw lobster tails.

Using a sharp knife, cut down the centre of the shell, through the meat, but not through the undershell. Spread tail open, butterfly style.

Combine melted butter, lemon juice, lemon peel, ginger, paprika, garlic salt and pepper to taste. Brush mixture over lobster.

Place tails on foil on the grill, undershell down.

Grill for 15 to 20 minutes or until meat loses its translucency and can be flaked easily with a fork.

Loosen meat from shell, then brush with butter mixture before serving.

Stuffed Salmon or White Fish with Tomatoes
Serves 8 (photo, page 32)

4-5 lbs.	whole salmon	2-2.5 kg
1	bunch parsley	1
3	bay leaves	3
	1/2 bunch fresh coriander, chopped	
3	cloves garlic, chopped	3
1	bunch green onions, chopped	1
2/3 cup	stale bread, in small cubes	150 mL
6	tomatoes	6
1 tsp.	thyme	5 mL
3	peppers	3
1/4 cup	olive oil	50 mL
1/2 tsp.	white pepper	2 mL
	salt	

Scale, clean and wash fish.

Gently remove the middle bone.

In a large pot, cook the middle bone with 2 cups water, stalk of parsley, bay leaves, salt and pepper. Bring to a boil and then simmer while preparing stuffing. (This results in a court bouillon.) Strain before using.

Blend coriander, chopped parsley, garlic, green onions, stale bread, 2 peeled and diced tomatoes, salt and pepper. Blend well.

Stuff fish with mixture, and sew shut.

In an oven-proof dish, arrange 4 peeled and sliced tomatoes in a single layer. Sprinkle with thyme and salt.

Place stuffed fish on top and sprinkle with olive oil. Cover with sheet of aluminum foil.

Bake in a 400°F (200°C) oven for a total of 35 - 45 minutes. After 20 minutes, pour court bouillon over fish, remove foil and return to oven.

After a further 20 minutes, check using a toothpick. If, after piercing the fish, the toothpick comes out dry, the fish is cooked.

Serve with rice and vegetables.

Frisco Crab

Serves 4

1 lb.	crab meat, cooked	500 g
	lettuce or trimmed spinach	
1 cup	mayonnaise	250 mL
1/3 cup	35% cream	75 mL
1/4 cup	chili sauce	50 mL
1/4	green pepper, seeded and chopped	1/4
4	green onions, chopped	4
2 tbsp.	mustard pickle or piccalilli	30 mL
1 tbsp.	lemon juice	15 mL
	salt	
	dash of Worcestershire sauce	
4	eggs, hard boiled and sliced	4
4	tomatoes, sliced	4
	parsley or olives	

Pick over the crab, removing any pieces of shell.

Arrange the crab on a bed of lettuce or spinach leaves on a large platter or on individual salad plates.

For the sauce, combine the next nine ingredients in a bowl and season to taste.

Spoon sauce over the crab and garnish with slices of egg, tomatoes and parsley or olives.

Metric in the Kitchen

For your convenience and to accommodate your most comfortable method of cooking, you will find measurement conversions here. As a general rule, however, try to avoid converting your recipes from one measurement type to the other. It often doesn't work as well as using the measurement type—imperial or metric—that is cited for specific ingredients in each recipe. For that reason, don't throw away your "old" measuring utensils, but do purchase a set of metric measuring utensils for the many metric recipes being published today.

Volume measurements

The most common measurement in metric recipes is the millilitre, or mL for short. Your measuring spoons and cups, for both liquid and dry measure, will be in mL measure. Here's how it works:

    1 tsp. (teaspoon) = 5 mL
    1 tbsp. (tablespoon) = 15 mL
    1 cup = 250 mL

Large volumes of 1,000 mL or more are measured in litres, or L for short. Milk, for example, is sold in litre containers. Also, your baking pans and casseroles will be measured by volume, in litres.

1 fl. oz. (fluid ounce) = 28.41 mL
1 pt. (pint) = 570 mL (or 0.57 L)
1 qt. (quart) = 1.14 L
1 Imperial gallon = 4.54 L

1 mL = 0.04 fl. oz.
1 L = 1.75 pt.
1 L = 0.88 qt.
1 L = 0.22 Imperial gallon

Length measurements

The metric measurement for length most often used in the kitchen is the centimetre, or cm for short.

1 in. (inch) = 2.54 cm
1 ft. (foot) = 0.30 m (metre)
1 yd. (yard) = 0.91 m
1 mi. (mile) = 1.61 km (kilometre)

1 cm = 0.39 in.
1 m - 3.28 ft.
1 m = 1.09 yd.
1 km = 0.62 mi.

Weight measurements

Grams and kilograms, g and kg respectively for short, are the metric measurements for weighing such foods as meat, fish, poultry, cheese, butter and cereals.

    1 oz. (ounce) = 28.35 g
    1 lb. (pound) = 0.45 kg
    1 ton = 0.91 t (tonne)

    1 g = 0.04 oz.
    1 kg = 2.21 lb.
    1 t = 1.10 ton

Try to remember:
    100 g weighs a little less than 1/4 lb.
    250 g weighs a little more than 1/2 lb.
    500 g weighs a little more than 1 lb.
    1,000 g (1 kg) weighs a little more than 2 lbs.

Temperature

Temperature in metric is measured in degrees Celcius or °C. To convert °F (Fahrenheit) to °C, use the formula below:

    (°F minus 32) x (5/9) = °C
    eg. (212 °F - 32) x (5/9) = 100 °C

Notes

Notes